1. HOW GANESHA GOT HIS ELE

One day, Parvati was sitting in her bedchamber.

Suddenly the door was flung open.

Thereupon a fierce fight began between Shiva and the young boy.

"What is this? None of my weapons is proving to be effective against the lad!"

He angrily chopped off the boy's head.

The sounds of the fight reached Parvati's ears.

She came to the door and her eyes fell on the boy's still form.

"What have you done to my son?"

Parvati began weeping.

"Please forgive me! Don't cry!"

"I must avenge this cruel act - what harm did my son do?"

She created an army of Goddesses all armed with weapons.

"Go and fight!"

Shiva's followers, the Ganas, fought in vain, but fell soon.

Then Shiva said to his remaining followers.

"Go into the world and bring me the head of the first creature sleeping in the wrong position."

The Ganas entered a jungle and saw a baby elephant.

"Look, the creature is sleeping with its head towards the north, that is, the wrong position! Let us cut off its head!"

"But it is an animal's head!"

"Never mind!"

The Chief Gana cut off the baby elephant's head to take back.

7

2. GANESHA'S VAHANA

Once there was a powerful Asura called 'Gajasura' as he had the head of an elephant.

"I wish to become great by defeating the Devas, my enemies!"

So, Gajasura performed severe penance to Shiva for years.

His prayers were answered at last.

"So be it!"

"Lord, please grant me the boon that the only creature who can slay me should be as dark-faced as I am!"

Gajasura then began a reign of terror and wreaked destruction wherever he went.

The Devas could bear it no longer.

"Lord, please save us from Gajasura! He is creating havoc!"

"I can do nothing, as Gajasura has obtained a boon from Lord Shiva that only a dark-faced creature can slay him. But, I have a suggestion. Approach Ganesha for help!"

The Devas went to Ganesha and told him their tale of woe about Gajasura.

"Do not worry any more! I shall help you!"

"What! Have you come to fight with me?"

Gajasura laughed when he saw the pot-bellied elephant-headed Ganesha.

A fierce battle between the elephant-faced asura and the elephant-headed Ganesha began, watched by the Devas.

"I must attack him differently and take him by surprise!"

Suddenly Ganesha attacked the asura with his tusk.

"Oh! I am losing all the powers I had obtained!"

He changed into a 'mooshika' (mouse) and tried to run away.

But Ganesha leaped on to the mouse's back.

"Please forgive me for my wrongs!"

"All right, I forgive you as you are truly sorry! From today you shall be my Vahana!"

This shows that egoism (represented by the mouse) which enters the mind stealthily can be controlled by divine wisdom.

3. WHY GANESHA HAS A BROKEN TUSK

The sage Vyasa, the author of the Vedas, was the son of the great sage Parasara.

Once, the beginning of a poem occurred to Vyasa as he sat in meditation.

He prayed to Brahma, the Creator.

"I have thought of an epic poem. But I cannot think of anyone who can take down my dictation!"

"O sage! I advise you to pray to Ganesha, the God of Wisdom, and ask him to be your scribe!"

So, Vyasa began meditating on Ganesha.

2a

But he had no writing material. So, he broke off one of his ivory tusks and used it as a stylus.

Sage Vyasa often composed difficult verses and used the time Ganesha took to understand to compose more verses.

Thus was born the longest epic known to the world - THE MAHABHARATA.

4. HOW GANESHA HUMBLED KUBERA'S PRIDE

Kubera, the Lord of Wealth once went to Mt.Kailasa to pay homage to Shiva and Parvati. Ganesha and Kartikeya were present too.

"My Lord, I have come to invite you to a grand feast which I have arranged specially for you tomorrow. Please attend it with the Goddess Parvati, Lord Ganesha and Lord Kartikeya!"

"A feast! How wonderful! Please order as many dishes to be cooked as possible!"

Alakaapuri, Kubera's legendary city, wore a festive look.

"Welcome! Where are your parents and brother?"

"They could not come, hence sent me instead. I am very hungry! Please take me to the dining hall!"

Kubera led the way and thought.

"How much can a young boy like Ganesha eat?"

"Bring more food! The plates are empty.

Kubera watched as Ganesha began eating.

The plates became empty again.

Kubera was beginning to look worried.

"I will ask the cooks to prepare more food!"

"I am still hungry!"

Ganesha ate the freshly-cooked food in no time.

"I am still hungry!" What do you have for me to eat?"

"Bring all the vegetables and fruits from the store rooms!"

Kubera ordered his cooks.

Ganesha ate them all.

"I shall have all the uncooked rice, grains and dhals too!"

"All the vessels in the kitchen and store rooms are empty!"

The cooks whispered to each other.

"Is there anything left? Ah yes! The firewood!"

Ganesha said loudly and ate the stacks of firewood.

"I must teach Kubera a lesson for trying to impress us all with his wealth!"

"My Lord, there is nothing left in the entire city!"

Kubera prayed to Lord Shiva.

"O Lord! This is a good lesson for me. I wished to impress you with my wealth, but Ganesha has humbled me!"

"Go and pray to Ganesha to forgive you!"

Kubera prostrated before Ganesha.

"O Ganesha! Please forgive me for trying to show off instead of showing true devotion!"

"Always remember, I can be satisfied with a single fruit if it is offered to me with devotion!"

5. WHY GANESHA CURSED THE MOON

Once Ganesha attended a feast where he was served a variety of sweets. His favourite sweet was 'modaka' and he filled his large belly with as much modaks as possible. Ganesha's vahana, the mooshika, too, nibbled at the modaks.

"I must go home now as I am feeling full!"

Ganesha set off home. But he felt so full that he could walk very slowly. He saw a snake and tied it around his bulging belly.

The moon who was shining in the sky, saw all this and began laughing.

"Ha! Ha! what a funny sight!"

Ganesha became very angry.

"O Chandra! You shall be punished for laughing at me, the God of Wisdom! Whoever looks at you on this night will be accused of a crime he has not committed!"

"I realise my mistake. Please forgive me and take back the curse!"

"As you have realised your mistake, I forgive you. But I cannot undo the curse. However, a person who is unjustly blamed can get relief by seeing you the next night!"

That is why it is said that it is unlucky to see the moon on Chathurthi day in the month of Bhadrapada.

6. THE SYAMANTAKA GEM

Even the great Lord Krishna could not escape Ganesha's curse....

Once, there was a King called Satrajeet in Dwaraka. He had received a precious gem called 'Syamantaka' from the Sun God, which could give limitless wealth.

"Use it for the welfare of the people!"

Lord Krishna said when Satrajeet showed him the Syamantaka gem.

But Satrajeet ignored the advice and locked the gem away after using it for himself.

One day, Satrajeet's brother, Prasena, wore the Syamantaka gem around his neck when he went for hunting. When Prasena did not return, Satrajeet said to Krishna.

"You have killed Prasena and have stolen the Syamantaka gem!"

Lord Krishna was very upset and went to the forest to search for Prasena. He came upon Prasena's dead body and the carcass of a lion some yards away. But the Syamantaka gem was missing.

Krishna followed a trail and came to a cave where he saw a beautiful maiden wearing the Syamantaka gem. He soon learned that her father, Jambavanta, had killed the lion and had given the gem to his daughter.

When Jambavanta realised that Krishna was none other than Sri Rama, he said...

"Please take the Syamantaka, my Lord!"

Krishna returned the Syamantaka gem to Satrajeet who in turn gave his daughter, Sathyabama, in marriage to Lord Krishna.

Lord Krishna met Narada who said...

"Your bad luck was caused because you accidentally saw the moon's reflection in a pail of water on Chathurthi Day!"

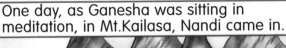

One day, as Ganesha was sitting in meditation, in Mt.Kailasa, Nandi came in.

"My Lord, all the Devas have come to meet you!"

"I will see them."

"Why are you all so worried?"

"O Lord! The demon Analasura is harassing us all greatly!"

"We are all afraid of approaching Analasura as he breathes fire from his mouth. So, if anyone dares to go near Analasura, he is reduced to ashes."

"Analasura is protected by a boon to belch fire and burn whoever opposes him!"

"Please destroy Analasura before he burns us all!"

"All right, I shall help you. Do not worry any more!"

Ganesha approached Analasura with a huge army. But the asura belched fire and burnt up the entire army. Ganesha became furious.

A terrible battle began between Ganesha and Analasura.

"Analasura cannot be destroyed by any weapon. So, I have to do something surprising!"

He caught the asura with his trunk and swallowed him.

Analasura had been swallowed alive by Ganesha. He began moving inside Ganesha's stomach.

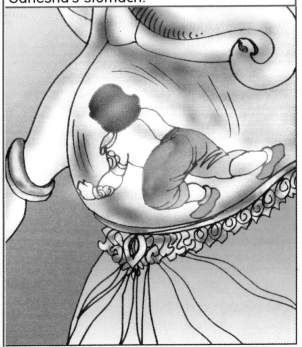

As a result, Ganesha's stomach felt as if it was on fire.

"Oh, help! My stomach is on fire!"

The Devas were all aghast.

"We must do something quickly and put out the fire in Lord Ganesha otherwise he will be burnt to death!"

"Let us pour cold water on Lord Ganesha. It may stop the burning."

They brought Ganga water and poured it on Ganesha.

"Nothing has happened! The fire is still burning!"

The Devas brought snow and ice from the mountain peaks and placed them on Ganesha's head.

"It is of no use. The fire is still burning."

The Devas placed the cool crescent moon on Ganesha's head. (so, he became known as 'Balachandar')

"The fire is still burning."

Then a sage brought a handful of 'darba' grass and placed them on Ganesha's head.

"Ah! Now the burning has gone completely. Analasura has been destroyed!"

"From now, those who want to obtain my blessing and favour, should worship me with 'darba' grass!"

King Kavera had no children. So, he renounced kingship and went to meditate to Lord Brahma for progeny.

"What do you want?"

"I want a son!"

"Kavera, you cannot have children. But, I shall reward you with this baby girl as I am pleased with your devotion!"

The girl, named Kaveri, grew up into a lovely maiden.

"I shall do penance in this Sahya mountain till I get a worthy husband!"

At that very moment, all the Devas had gathered in the Himalayas to attend the marriage of Shiva and Parvati. So, the Southern areas tilted upwards and the North sank lower. Shiva called the great sage Agasthya.

"Proceed to the Pothiya mountain and stay there for the welfare of the land till my marriage. I shall grant you divine sight to see the marriage.

"As you command, O Lord!"

Sage Agasthya went South. As he performed Shiva worship in the Sahya mountain, he met Kaveri.

"O maiden! Why are you doing penance?"

"May your wish be fulfilled!"

"Lord Brahma gave me as a boon to my father, Kavera. I want a worthy husband and that is why I am doing penance. Please bless me so that I may succeed."

Agasthya sprinkled water from his 'kamandalam' (water-jug) on Kaveri.

"May part of you become a holy river and stay in my 'kamandalam'. I shall marry the other part of you.

At that time, there was drought in the Chola Kingdom. Indra, who was worshipping Lord Shiva, was approached by Narada.

"O King of the Devas, please can you pray to Vighneshwara and get him to release the river Kaveri which is in Agasthya's 'kamandalam'? The parched land will become green again!"

"I shall do so at once!"

24

Indra worshipped Lord Vighneshwara who appeared before him.

"What can I do for you?"

"O Lord! Vighneshwara! The river Kaveri is being held in Agasthya's 'kamandalam'. Please find a way to release her for the welfare of the drought-hit land!"

Lord Vighneshwara went as a crow to the place where Agasthya was meditating and sat on his 'kamandalam'.

"Shoo!"

The crow flew away, but upset the 'kamandalam'. Kaveri flowed out at once.

Agasthya looked around and saw a strange boy, who ran off.

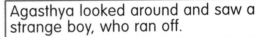

"Hey, boy! Come here! Who are you! I shall give you a sound knock on your head!"

Suddenly the boy turned into Lord Vighneshwara.

"O Lord! I wanted to catch you and give you a knock on your head without knowing who you were! How can I remove this sin?"

Agasthya knocked his own head with his knuckles in remorse. Lord Vighneshwara filled Agasthya's 'kamandalam' with some Kaveri water.

"Thank you O Lord! for teaching mankind a way to obtain your grace!"

"O sage! Go to the Pothiya hill and let the Kaveri flow there. If others knock their own heads with their knuckles like you, all ignorance will be removed and they will become wise!"

Agasthya then married Kaveri's other half who was known as Lopamudra, and lived happily with her.

It is largely believed that Lord Vighneshwara is responsible for bringing the Kaveri river to South India.

Ravana, the great Asura ruler of Lanka, was an ardent devotee of Lord Shiva. He never failed to offer prayers three times a day to Lord Shiva.

"I have learned that Lord Shiva has an 'atmalinga' which is a reflection of the Lord himself. If I could get hold of this Shivalinga, I shall become as powerful as Shiva!"

So, Ravana began to do severe penance to please Lord Shiva.

Lord Shiva appeared after Ravana's long penance.

"I am pleased by your devotion. Ask me for any boon!"

"O Lord Shiva! I wish to own your special 'atmalinga'!"

"So be it. But, King of Lanka, when you are returning home, you should not, on any account, put the 'atmalinga' on the ground. If it is placed on the ground, no one can remove it!"

"I shall be very careful!"

The Devas came to know that Ravana had obtained the 'atmalinga' from Lord Shiva.

"I am afraid of what can happen if he takes it to Lanka!"

They all went to Lord Ganesha.

"O Lord! No one will be able to defeat Ravana if he instals the 'atmalinga' of Lord Shiva in Lanka. What shall we do?

"I can understand what you mean, and shall see that Ravana's plan does not succeed. So, do not worry!"

Ravana was returning to Lanka with the 'atmalinga' in his hands. Twilight was approaching.

"O! It is time for my evening prayers to Lord Shiva."

Ravana was near the seashore and there was no one in sight.

"What shall I do? If I put the 'atmalinga' down, it will remain in this place!"

Ravana suddenly saw a small boy, who was really Lord Ganesha.

"Boy, please can you hold this Shivalinga for me while I offer prayers to God? I will come back quickly!"

"All right! But it will be dark soon and I must go home. I shall wait for some time and call you three times. If you do not come, I will put the Shivalinga on the ground and go away!"

Ravana placed the 'atmalinga' in the boy's hand and walked away to pray Lord Shiva.

This was the chance Ganesha was waiting for. He let some time pass and then shouted.

"Please come soon! My hands are aching!"

"Give me a little more time to finish my prayers!"

"I know the power of this 'atmalinga' and I also know that Lord Shiva has said to Ravana. So, I will wait for some more time."

"I cannot bear the heavy weight of this Shivalinga anymore. So, I am putting it on the ground.

Ravana came running up when he heard the boy's words to find that the 'atmalinga' was on the ground. The boy had vanished.

Ravana tried to uproot the 'atmalinga'. The more he pulled at it, the longer it grew and resembled a cow's ear.

The place came to be called 'Gokarna'. The Lord here is known as 'Mahabaleshwara' and has a huge temple dedicated to him.

10. LORD VISHNU'S DILEMMA

Young Ganesha was very much attracted by Lord Vishnu's Chakra. He thought that it was a toy. Once he grabbed it playfully and put it into his mouth.

Lord Vishnu was very troubled.

"What shall I do? How will I get it back from him - he is so strong!"

He pondered for some time.

"I know! I shall make him laugh. He will shake and quiver so much with mirth that the Chakra may fall out from his mouth!"

Lord Vishnu caught hold of his own ears with his hands. Then he bent down and straightened up many times, performing the 'THOPPUKARNAM'.

On seeing this, Ganesha began laughing. The Chakra fell out of his mouth and Lord Vishnu grabbed it at once.

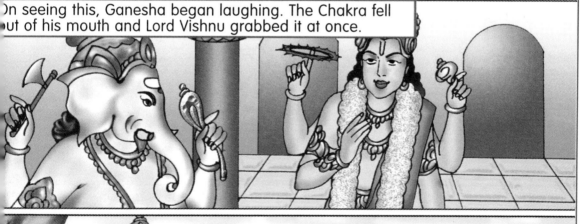

That is why we offer THOPPUKARNAM to please Lord Ganesha, it is said.

11. WHY ARE COCONUTS BROKEN FOR GANESHA

Once Ganesha said to Lord Shiva.

"Give me your head as a sacrifice."

To symbolise this great sacrifice, Lord Shiva created the coconut, with its 3 holes (to represent his 3 eyes) and broke it before Ganesha. Though the coconut has a hard exterior, it has a soft kernel inside.

Ganesha's head denotes Wisdom. The 2 big ears are receptive to Vedanta and Truth. The 3 eyes represent Surya, Chandra and Agni. The single ivory tusk represents two sides of the same coin - happiness/sadness, poverty/wealth, sweetness/bitterness. The big stomach denotes that everything is under control, especially one's ego.

Ten names of Ganesha

1. Vighneshwara
2. Ganesha
3. Ganapathy
4. Gajapathy
5. Ekadanta
6. Vinayaka
7. Pillayar
8. Gajamukha
9. Heramba
10. Lambodara